THE CHOSEN ONE

Brittany C. Carson

Copyright © 2016 by Brittany C. Carson
First Edition 2016

All rights reserved. No part of this book may be reproduced or transmitted in any form or by any means, electronic or mechanical, including photocopying, recording or by any information storage and retrieval system, without written permission from the author, except for the inclusion of brief quotations in a review.
Library of Congress Cataloging-in-Publication Data

Brittany C. Carson
The Chosen One
Edited by: Driadonna Roland
Published by: Brittany C. Carson

Library of Congress Control Number: 2015921500
ISBN: 9780692610398
ISBN 10: 0692610391
10 9 8 7 6 5 4 3 2 1
Printed in the United States of America

Note: This book is intended only as a real life testimony of the life and times of Brittany C. Carson. Readers are advised to consult a professional relationship coach or counselor before making any changes in their love life. The reader assumes all responsibility for the consequences of any actions taken based on the information presented in this book. The information in this book is based on the author's research and experience. Every attempt has been made to ensure that the information is accurate; however, the author cannot accept liability for any errors that may exist. The facts and theories about life are subject to interpretation, and the conclusions and recommendations presented here may not agree with other interpretations.
Cover Design by NickRichgfx

Visit me at www.BrittanyCCarson.com

TABLE OF CONTENTS

Introduction		v
Chapter 1	July Arrival	1
Chapter 2	Being A Child	5
Chapter 3	What Really Caught My Attention?	14
Chapter 4	Dare to Be Different	17
Chapter 5	Growing Up in a Rough Neighborhood	23
Chapter 6	Sight of Abusive Acts	35
Chapter 7	Free Will	40
Chapter 8	Reoccurring Pain	45
Chapter 9	Spiritual Awakening (Pivotal Point)	62
Chapter 10	God's Work	72
Chapter 11	Building and Adjusting	83
Chapter 12	Knowledge Is Power	89
In Closing		99

INTRODUCTION

I have been holding back my life story for quite some time now. I had to write this book to let people know that you should never judge people by their cover. Others have assumed that I suppose I am perfect or better than other people. No one is perfect, not even me. In this book, I will tell you just how not perfect I am. I am just a regular person with a real story. The experiences we have turn into our stories; those are our teachings. You can gain so much knowledge from the experiences that you encounter when you learn from them. In this book I am going to be real with you. I want to share my spiritually awakened journey with you, the journey of me being aware of everything around me. I went from having a closed mind to opening my mind to the different things in the world. I look around and see unhappy people all the time. They are damaged and broken. They have no idea where to start to put the broken pieces back together in order to heal themselves. In this book I will talk about how I went from being damaged to being healed. I became happier in my life. I will speak the truth no matter what others think. The truth will set you free.

Becoming a better you will bring peace and happiness into your life. I have been at my lowest point in my life, and if I made it from where I was I know that anybody else can too. I made many mistakes before learning from my experiences. I still make mistakes today; we are only human, that is what we do until we get it right. It is a good thing to make mistakes so you can know that everything you do might not come out right the first time. You can learn from them and get it right the next time. People see how I am now, but they do not know where I come from. They do not know how much I have been through. I want to share my story with you in the hopes that you can be the one to influence others by reading my story. I allowed God to come into my life to lead me in the right direction. He has me on the right path that I am supposed to be on. I am more confident, calm, wise, strong, patient, humble, and happy. I am no longer lost in my life. I have God and my angels by my side at all times. I have been chosen to be a servant of God. Everyone has a purpose here on earth, whether you believe it or not. I hope my story can help you on your journey if you are looking to become a better person or if you may be lost in life trying to find your way.

CHAPTER 1
JULY ARRIVAL

In the springtime of 1990, the doctor predicted that my mom was going to have a baby boy. My parents were planning to get an abortion since she already had a child at 18 years old. The first child my mom had was my older sister. My mother got pregnant with her by someone she dated before meeting my dad. So now my mom would be having two kids by the age of 19. When she was in the 12th grade that is when she had my sister. She decided to drop out of high school because trying to do both was a tough challenge for her. Before she got pregnant with me she was able to go to night school to get her high school diploma. Once she found out she was having another child my parents went ahead and decided to have me. My parents knew they had to step up as adults even though they were still young. The news was spread around to my family about her having another baby. My parents wanted a baby boy. Like most families do, they buy items for the baby before they are birthed so when the baby comes it will have items. Both sides of my family started to buy baby boy items before I was born. On July 12, 1990, a Thursday morning in Spartanburg Regional located in Spartanburg, South Carolina, I was born. Although the doctor predicted that my mom was having a boy, they found out when I was delivered that she had a girl. Come to find out the umbilical cord was covering up my private area, so they assumed I was going to be a boy. After everyone saw that I was a girl, I was named Brittany C. Carson. I was born seven pounds and eight ounces. I was a healthy and beautiful baby. The doctor said that I had a heart murmur at birth, so they monitored it closely. The doctors knew that I was strong enough to breathe on my own; they did not consider it a threat to me. Meanwhile, all the clothes, toys, and items that were bought for me were actually for a boy, so my family had to take all that stuff back and replace it with girl items. When I got a little older I remember asking my mom why she named me Brittany. She said, "I did not name you, I was in too much pain at the time to name you, so I let your aunts on your dad's side name you." I guess I had to settle for that.

As I said before, my mom dropped out of school because she had to become an adult faster than she thought. She went back to school to get her high school diploma. My dad was able to graduate high school. At the moment I was his first child. When I was born my mom was 19 and my dad was 17 years old. My mom told me stories about how she and my dad met. She said that she had a class with him in high school and all he used to do was joke around. My mom was the shy, quiet type of person, and smiled a lot. I can say that I get some of my ways from both of them. My mom is an introvert and dad is an extrovert. I am more of an introvert, but have some extrovert ways about me. I have wondered to myself a few times how did they become attracted to one another. It had to be the reason why they came together was for the making of me.

My parents becoming adults at a young age took a lot of learning, adjusting, changing, and sacrificing. They had to start working jobs immediately so they could take care of my sister and me. My grandparents on both of my parents' sides and some other family members helped my parents when they needed it. I remember being dropped off at a few of my family members' houses sometimes to be watched while my parents were at work. They were working at low-paying jobs, so times got rough for us. I always knew that whenever my parents needed assistance with anything my grandfather on my mother's side was there no matter what. If he was at work or could not help my parents at the moment my other grandparents would assist. He is a great man. He supported me, taught me a lot of things, and always encouraged me to do the right things. He was also known as "the ladies' man," as some people would call it. I met a lot of different women when I was younger through him. I only remember about three of the women's names. Everything was not so sweet just because my parents had some supporters. They still had to go get things on their own for the sake of their kids. They are great parents and have always done the best they could for us. I would not trade them for anyone else in the world. My birth changed their lives and made them grow into adults. As they were growing I continued to grow also.

CHAPTER 2
BEING A CHILD

I remember being an energetic, rough, hard-headed, intelligent, smart-mouthed, and playful little girl. I just wanted to explore, mess with everything, and play — the things that most kids do. I was small, but strong and tough. I would play in the dirt, jump from couch to couch in the house, and run wild. I would wake up in the morning and do the same thing over again. Doing those things everyday was all that I wanted to do. I was not in daycare yet, so I would stay at my babysitter's, grandmother's, and great-grandparents' house when my parents were gone to work. When my dad was not at work we would spend time together a lot. We would wrestle and play all the time. As a toddler and preschooler I spent more time with him. My mom was working a second-shift job when I started going to daycare at the YMCA. When I attended the YMCA I enjoyed swimming, playing basketball, playing with other kids, and participating in other activities. I did not get to see her as much as I wanted to until the morning time. That was when she was waking me up to go to daycare. When she got off at night I was already in bed. I understood that she was a hard-working woman.

Both of my parents experienced a lot of tough times. When I was around 2 years old my sister was hit by a car. She was 3 years old. She ran out in the front of a car and was hit by an older man. My mom told me the story when I got old enough to understand; this was devastating. I felt sorry for my sister and what she went through. The doctor did not know how she was still living and they were surprised that she made it through that tragic accident. My mom was not on the scene when it happened because she was at work. My sister was with someone on her dad's side of the family. The people at the scene told my mom that my sister's small body slid under the car after she had been hit. Her leg was broken in half. She had burn marks on her face and legs from the oil dripping from underneath the car when she was hit. She had to stay in the hospital for a month. My family was by her side the whole time she was going through this pain.

The Chosen One

My mom told me that her nerves were tore up that something like this had happened to her daughter. My family and I were very thankful that she survived that accident.

By the ages of 4 to 6, people would say that I was rough around the edges. I was always doing things that I was not supposed to be doing. I stayed getting in trouble, then getting a whooping for it. I was the one you would have called adventurous. Outside at my great-grandparents' house on my mom's side of the family I would climb trees, jump from one tree to the other, play with the water hose, and just do things that I did not know would get me in trouble. I did what other kids would be doing at that age range. I guess because I was a girl people expected me to act and behave like a girl. I was always the one getting injured in some kind of way. In my childhood my parents stayed at the doctor with me. Either I was getting stitches or Band-Aids. Those things never stopped me from doing anything I wanted to do. I was an outside type of person, could not stand to be kept in the house. I have always wanted to just be free. There were rules I was supposed to have been going by, but I did not go by them. During this age range I discovered that basketball was what I liked. I saw people on TV doing it. I even watched my dad play with his friends while I sat on the side at the park.

Between the ages of 6 to 9, I was still the same playful, tomboyish, and adventurous little girl. I was getting in trouble at my elementary school like every week. I was sent to the principal's office a lot. The school would call my parents so that they could send me home. I was sent home with bad notes all the time. My mom did not really punish me as much for the things I got in trouble for. If she did she would pinch me. Some people think that may not have hurt, but it did. My dad was the one who would punish me by giving me whoopings. Most of the whoopings I think I did not deserve. I was still a child that would do things just like other kids were doing. I do not think I should have been punished for some of the stuff. If I were disciplined in another way it would have been better. He would whoop me with leather belts, switches off the tree (which is a small branch), or his hands. Sometimes he would hit me in the back of my head with his hand if I was doing something that he did not like. Sometimes you could see the print of his hands on my body after I was punished. The belt and switch prints would show up on my body as welts. At times I would sit and cry while looking at the red welts on my body. Going through these things made me want to move from home but I was too young at the time.

My father was whooped by his parents a lot in his childhood. He mentioned it to me a few times when we were taking a trip down memory lane. That was the only way he knew how to discipline me because that was the way he was raised. Being abused was passed down to him. I would say it is a generational curse. Emotionally, mentally, verbally, and physically it would hurt me every time I was being punished. Emotionally my feelings were hurt. Mentally I was beginning to form fear and hate toward my father. Verbally I was becoming tormented by the profanity or language he would use toward me. Physically the whoopings would hurt my body and was sore afterward. After my punishment I would go back to do the same thing again that got me in trouble the first time. I feel like the whoopings did not discipline me, they just scared me. I was gaining a dislike toward him for doing that to me. I cannot blame him because he did not know any better. He was not aware that the abusive habits he experienced growing up were being passed down to me from him. When he was giving me whoopings he was probably thinking about the way he used to be whooped as a child. Anger was taken out on me from his past issue and what he was dealing with in life at that moment.

Growing up I had hatred in my heart and anger toward him. I could not understand at the moment why would he whoop me that way. Now I strongly believe before I was born my dad wanted to have a boy. He did not get to live his dreams out the way he wanted to, so having a boy to raise could allow him to live his dreams through him. Things did not work out that way, so he ended up with a girl. Fathers are usually tougher on their son than they are on their daughter. He was tough on me as if I were a boy. The way I was being whooped it seemed like a boy would be tough enough to take those punishments, not a girl. A lot was taken out on me, but he did not realize it. Later on in life I had to understand the generational issue, what he went through as a child, what he had dealt with in life, and forgive him.

I continued to get in trouble for my behavior in school. The teachers were complaining that I was extremely hyperactive, not paying attention in class, and not behaving like the other students were. So, I would get in trouble for being who I really was. It was something that I could not control as a child. The elementary school that I was going to made my behavior sound 10 times worse to my parents. My parents had to take me to mental health to get a few tests done. When I took the tests I passed with flying colors. I did not have a mental health problem. The only thing I had a problem with was being hyperactive. Hyperactive means that I was showing that I was constantly active and sometimes I may have had disruptive behavior. People would also call this kind of behavior Attention Deficit Hyperactivity Disorder, or ADHD. That is a chronic condition in which one could have attention difficulty, hyperactivity, and impulsiveness. This is a very common disorder around the world for kids to be diagnosed with. The doctors were telling my parents that the disorder could last for years or be lifelong. This is a disorder that cannot be cured, but treatment may help. So I was diagnosed with ADHD and prescribed to take medication for it. The medicine I had to take every day for this disorder was called Adderall. It is a substitute medication for Ritalin.

Once I started taking my medication every day I was put in resource class, but I was still taking regular classes also. Resource class is a separate, remedial classroom in a school where students with learning and educational disabilities were placed for a certain amount of time throughout the school day. In that class I was given direct specialized instructions, assistance with assignments, and one-on-one time with my teacher. My teacher was a nice person. She showed me that she cared about me. I cannot remember her name because it has been so many years ago. I would go to that class every day, then go to my regular classes. My behavior and grades started to get better. The medication I was on did have some kind of good effect on me. After a while my resource teacher explained to my parents that I did not belong in that type of class. She told them that I did not have a learning disability. My behavior was no longer a problem. So they removed me from that class, then I was just taking regular classes all day. The elementary school I was attending made me go to summer school to take classes. They figured that my behavior in class was holding me back from the lessons being taught in the classroom. In the summertime they made me make up for it. I felt like it was not fair.

A few months of being on that medication was taking a toll on me. When I was at home my parents and everyone who knew me well saw that I was not the Brittany they were used to. I was not being myself. It was like the medication was sucking all the energy out of me. I was not interacting with others. I slept more than I would usually sleep throughout the day. On top of that I was losing weight. I was not fat as a child, but I was big boned. That medication made me look small and sick. My teacher was sending notes home to my mom saying I was sleeping in class. The medication was too strong for me; it was affecting my whole life and it was changing me as a child. I was not able to be that playful and adventurous person I always was. I believed the elementary school I was attending did not like me or something. They wanted me on that medication because they could not control me. When I got on the medication they were still complaining about me. My mom was not getting a medical check for me because I was diagnosed with ADHD. It was like the system was getting over on us. The social security income (SSI) system would not allow me to get a check for having ADHD because I was taking regular classes along with a resource class. My mom tried to get approved two times, but she was denied. The money would have been a big help for my family. At the time my parents were in and out of different jobs trying to make a living. Times got hard and sometimes they would have to get loans in order to take care of us. My mom ended up taking me off of the medication because it had affected me so much that I was not being myself anymore. My family wanted to see me as the playful, good, happy, and interactive person they knew me as. Now that the medication was gone I was back to myself.

CHAPTER 3

WHAT REALLY CAUGHT MY ATTENTION?

Having ADHD came out to be a good thing for me. I found a way to use that energy I had. I discovered that I really liked basketball at the age of 6. I would watch basketball on TV all the time. I would see people playing it all the time. That caught my attention to play basketball and to be a basketball player. I remember my parents buying me a basketball with the basketball goal to go with it; it was the Little Tikes basketball goal for little kids. That was usually sold at Toys R Us, Wal-Mart, and many other stores that sold toys. I fell in love with that basketball goal. I would play on it almost every day. Wherever

The Chosen One

I went the basketball and goal were going with me. I tried to play like the people I saw on television. I wanted to play like the basketball players or even better than them. I had the energy, attitude, and some of the skills to start off being a basketball player. I remember my mom sharing with me that I would bug her every day about wanting to play basketball on a team. Money was tight for my parents, so they really did not have the funds to put me on a basketball team at the time. Some way my mom and grandfather came up with the money for me to play on a team. They knew playing basketball was something that I really wanted to do. Playing basketball would give me the opportunity to burn off all that energy I had always had in me. At the age of 8 I started playing basketball for a community center. I was so happy to be playing basketball; it was something that I loved to do.

After that first year I started playing basketball I continued to play every year. When I started it was something I could never stop doing. I have always been dedicated to the game of basketball. I have played for different community centers and church leagues. I remember my grandfather buying my first basketball shoes. They were called the Sheryl Swoopes. Those shoes were my everything. I loved the way they looked. I was able to play basketball in them real well. Sheryl Swoopes was a good basketball player in the WNBA who inspired me and other basketball players too. She was not my favorite basketball player though. When I started playing my favorite player was Allen Iverson, and he still is. He started playing in the NBA at a young age. I think he is an incredible basketball player. I imitated him a lot when it came to playing basketball. I imitated Allen Iverson because he played at the point guard position. I was playing the point guard position as well. He was my role model. I never really had a favorite basketball team, just individual basketball players. Playing basketball caught my attention. The love for the game stuck with me. I remember being in school doing an assignment that asked us what did we want to be when we grew up. I wrote down that I wanted to be a professional basketball player. I had no other plan or nothing else that I liked doing that had my heart. I had made my mind up that I would play for the WNBA or play overseas.

CHAPTER 4
DARE TO BE DIFFERENT

―✢―

From ages 10 to 12, I started to change a lot as most children do as they are growing up. I was getting a little older and started to transition my style. I was a tomboy, but I was still dressing as a girl. I really did not like it, but it was what my parents required me to do. I wanted to dress freely. I did not want to wear any tight clothing, but I wanted to be dressed nicely. I was the type of person who wanted to wear loose jeans, shorts, and T-shirts. I wanted to wear the nice tennis shoes like Nikes, Jordans, or Adidas. I never got a pair of Jordans because my parents did not have enough money for something that cost so much. I was still thankful for the shoes I got to wear though.

People began to admire and have crushes on me when I was in the fifth grade. I remember there was a young boy around my age that I had met through church. He liked me when we were going to church together. I went to church every Sunday with my close relatives at our family church. My mom and dad rarely went to church. But when they were younger their parents required them to go to church every Sunday, so they looked forward to my sister and me going to church. I got baptized at church one day. Baptism was performed by having my forehead dipped into water, then lifted back up. This act was symbolizing purification and admission to the Christian church. I figured I was on the right path by doing that. At the time I was so young I did not really know what it meant. In church I would participate in singing in the choir. I still enjoy singing now. I was the lead singer for some gospel songs we sang in the church. Some people on both sides of my families were great singers.

So the boy I mentioned who liked me that I was going to church with was a decent-looking, athletic, and cool person. We would lead gospel songs in church together. One day I remember he and I were sitting with the kids' choir waiting for the adult choir to sing. Someone tapped me on my shoulder, I turned around, and it was a note from him. The note said, "Do you like me, yes or no." This is quite hilarious to me as I sit and think about that day. On the letter I circled yes, then I sent to back to him by someone else. When he opened it I looked and saw a grin on his face. In my mind I was thinking, *What did I just agree to?* Since I circled yes that meant that we were going together I guess. The truth was that I did not know if I really liked him. I must have agreed to that note because people were saying all the time, "You two would be a cute couple." I was so young that I did not know anything about having a boyfriend. He and I never talked on the phone. The only time we would talk and see each other was when we were at church. Then, after like a month of being together we stopped going together. I think it was because we were growing up and apart. He started liking other people. I really was not interested in him. I was still a little girl, so my mind was on playing basketball, enjoying life, and being a kid.

While I was in the fifth grade, my mom got pregnant. She was pregnant by my dad with a baby boy. Now I had a baby brother and an older sister, which made me the middle child. I was excited about having a brother, but at the same time I was kind of scared. I knew that all the attention I was getting would be going to him now. I remember my mom telling me that I was jealous about him getting all the attention. I was jealous because I felt they were not going to pay me any attention like they used to.

I was not the baby anymore; my brother was now. Over the years I got over it. Now that it was a total of three of us my parents struggled more to put food on the table and clothes on our back.

As I continued to get older, in the sixth grade I started to dress boyish. I started wearing loose, boy clothing. I wanted to start wearing Timberland boots and tennis shoes that most boys would wear. I was still a tomboy, rough around the edges, playing basketball with boys most of my life at that point, and I started wearing my hair in braids; as some people call them "cornrows." I was cool. Well, I thought that I was a pretty cool person. I remember seeing one of my older cousins who would wear the new Jordans, Charles Barkleys, Timberlands, Scottie Pippens, Penny Hardaways, Deion Sanders, and a lot of other good-looking shoes. I loved his shoe collection. I wanted all of them. But when I would tell my parents about the shoes they were not having that. So every day when I went to my great-grandparents' house after school I would sneak to my cousin's room to try on all his shoes, even though I could not fit any of them because the shoes were like a size 10. I still fantasized about having my own pairs of shoes one day. I would put his shoes on and walk around upstairs in them. I looked down at the shoes with my small feet in them. The shoes made me feel like I was fly.

At around the age of 12 I had a lot of friends, boys and girls. I did not have a best friend. I got along with everyone most of the time. In school I did not get in any fights, had some disagreements but no physical altercations. I was the type of person with a good sense of humor, a pretty smile, my own style, athleticism, a pretty face, and a good personality. I have the same traits about me till this day.

At this time in my life I was not attracted to boys so much; I did not know why. I used to ask myself, *Why am I not attracted to boys?* I was not interested in them. I was attracted to girls. It was always said that boys are supposed to date girls. I know that it was mentioned in the Bible. But I was just attracted to girls. I found girls more attractive. Some of them had a very caring side, were easy to have conversations with, and had pretty faces, and many other things about them that attracted me. At this age I did not date anyone. I was still trying to figure out if it was real that I liked girls. I kept that thought in my mind and nobody knew. All I knew was that it was a bad thing for the same sex to go together. People would get picked on for dating the same sex. They would be called names. People dating the same sex have even been killed. That was the belief passed down from generation to generation. Having the attraction I had made me think that I was different from a lot of people around me. I dared to be different in many ways. I chose to dress a different way than most girls dressed and I was attracted to girls.

CHAPTER 5
GROWING UP IN A ROUGH NEIGHBORHOOD

Over the years as a child my family and I moved to different areas in Spartanburg, South Carolina. We have lived there most of our lives. Spartanburg is a very small city in the state of South Carolina. It is a good place to raise your kids and build a family. In Spartanburg most people know each other or who people may be related to. There are some good neighborhoods and some not so good. Growing up my family and I moved to multiple apartment complexes around Spartanburg. The first place I lived after I was born was with my mom at my great-grandparents' house on the south side of Spartanburg. My dad was living at his mother's house. So until the age of about 5 years old I lived at my great-grandparents' house. A lot of different family members lived there also. It was a house with only six rooms altogether; the attic was turned into three rooms. There were 12 people living in a small, six-bedroom house with tiny rooms. Yes, we were one big family. We slept on floors and couches, and we were crowded in the house. After we moved from there my mom, dad, sister, and I moved to another apartment complex.

Around the age of 8 years old we moved to one of the most violent and dangerous apartment complexes in Spartanburg. The name of the apartment complex was Cammie Clagett Courts. There were three different apartment complexes in one area, which included the one I lived in. All of them were public housing complexes. Public housing is a form of housing in which the property is owned by government authority. Basically you can say that I was living in the "ghetto" or "projects" as most people refer to it. As one whole neighborhood with the three complexes in the same area people called it Highland. This was the only place my parents could afford for us to live at the time. We lived in Highland for about 10 years. Most of my time growing up took place there. This was a place where the crime rate was known to be high, especially in the '90s. My parents were real protective of my sister and me. In the first two years of living in Highland they did not let us go outside much. My mom let us go over my great-grandparents' house so that we could play outside. My parents were afraid of someone harming us or something bad happening to us in the neighborhood. I was scared of the neighborhood at first also, so I did not care about playing outside there.

In those first couple of years of living there at night we would hear gunshots plenty of times a week. Even through the daytime we would hear gunshots going off. Soon as we heard the gunshots the walls would vibrate like the person was shooting right there in front of our apartment. We would have to lie on the floor and cover our heads and ears with our hands in order to make sure no bullets would come through the windows to strike one of us. The sounds of the gunshots were really loud. I was so afraid that at times I did not even sleep in my room. I would sleep on the couch or in my parents' room. I was not comfortable being alone in the apartment for the first couple of years we lived there.

Sometimes my mom did not have anyone to watch my sister and me in the summertime when we lived there, so she would take us to work with her. We were lucky that she worked in a hotel at that point. She would put us in a hotel room, then go do her job. We would help her clean up some of the rooms when her boss was not around. We were not supposed to be there. She had no choice but to take us with her. She did not want to leave us alone at home in Highland. At the time I was around the age of 11. I used to go swimming at the hotel a lot of times. Being able to watch cable there was great because we did not have some of the channels at home that the hotel had. We would get food from the breakfast bar in the morning. One day my mom and I experienced something that was life-threatening to us while we were at the hotel. I remember my mom telling me one evening to not come out of the hotel room she put us in. She told us that she was going to the front desk. We were not allowed to be by the front desk without her permission. The manager would usually be in that area a lot.

So one day, being who I am, I left out of the room while my sister stayed in the room. I had to ask my mom a question so I went to the front desk. Soon as I got to the front desk two men walked in with black ski masks, pointing a gun at everyone who was in there at the time. They were telling everyone to move to the back room. A robbery was taking place. My mom and I were a part of it with the other employees. They made us go in the back office, locked the doors to the building, and duct-taped our hands behind our back, as well as our mouths. They were yelling at us saying, "Stop crying or I will shoot you." They did not tape my mouth. I did as I was told, I stayed quiet, but inside I was heated. One of the robbers asked the lady who was working at the front desk that day what the code was to the safe. She replied that she did not know. That answer really made them mad. They kept asking for the money but nobody knew. The more they got mad they would point that chrome gun at people's heads. They did not point it at me. I saw them pointing the gun at my mom's head at one point. She had tears rolling down her face, mouth and hands duct-taped together. She was powerless and scared to death. She could not protect herself or me. The more I saw them doing that to my mom the madder I became. I wanted to stand up to them, but there was nothing I could do. I was sitting in that room like *This has to be a dream*, but it was real. I thought our lives were about to be ended right before our eyes. After they tried to get money out of the safe and did not succeed they finally gave up. Time was running out for them. They finally left without causing harm to anyone in the room. When they left I took the tape off my hands. I started helping take the tape off of the other people. We were so relieved but still afraid they would come back. The police were called to the scene. I do not think the robbers were captured by the police. That day opened my eyes. God was protecting all of us at that time and I truly feel blessed for that.

While still living in Highland we dealt with the struggle. There were times I would have to walk with my parents to the store or to the destination we were trying to get to. Some of those walks would be from where we stayed to across town. At that time they did not have a car. Sometimes we would ride on the city bus for transportation. In the apartments roaches were crawling on and in everything. Some people's apartments had roaches worse than ours. Over the years we started to see less of the roaches, so I did not have to worry about whether something was crawling on me. We lived off of food stamps. At times we would run out of food and drinks. Many days we ate ramen noodles, bologna, and peanut butter and jelly sandwiches. Bread was not even available at times, so we would eat the meat by itself if we had it. When we ran out of sodas and juice my mom would make Kool-Aid for us. I loved Kool-Aid, especially the red kind. The people who have drunk it know what the red kind is. I was very grateful for at least having some type of food to eat and drink.

With just one television we did not have cable at first, so a lot of days there were only three channels we could watch. Money was tight, times were rough, but my parents found a way to provide for us. We did not have central air until a couple of years after we moved into that apartment. We used to sleep in a hot apartment in the summertime. There was only one air conditioner that was sat in the window downstairs in the living room. The air downstairs did not make it upstairs, so it felt like we were melting upstairs. My mom could only afford the air conditioner for downstairs. Upstairs we would get the smaller fans, lift the windows up, and place them there, then turn them on to get some kind of breeze circulating. It was not a cool breeze until it got dark at night; in the daytime it was only heat flowing. My mom would keep the air conditioner on downstairs a certain amount of hours because it would make the electricity bill go up. For the wintertime we did have heat in the apartments, so that was a good thing.

Growing up in this neighborhood a lot of us dealt with police harassing us. I can understand that they were doing their job to catch the bad people. My friends and I would hang out together outside not causing anyone problems or harm. We would still get approached, being asked *Where are your IDs, Where do you live, Do you live in this neighborhood*, or *Why are you standing on this street?* They did not know who was doing wrong, so they tried to pick with everyone they saw. There were times when they would follow certain people to see what they were doing. There would be police who would jump out of vans or cars and jump out on kids or adults. They would be harassing them about drugs or if they thought they were doing something bad. Police would sit in their cars, taking pictures of us walking down the street, trying to catch someone doing wrong. I had a police officer come up to my friend and me asking us what our tattoos stood for. It was a tattoo on my hand with my initials. I know they just wanted to catch someone to put them in jail or thought we were gang members. If you looked like a thug pretty much they put you in the category of selling drugs or being up to no good. We dealt with a lot of stereotypes growing up in the projects.

As my sister and me were getting used to living in Highland we started making friends there. We got along with most kids we met there. The other kids would fight each other all the time in the neighborhood. I became friends with boys mostly because I would play basketball with them all the time. They were cool and fun and respected me. I became longtime friends with most of the boys I hung out with. We had each other's back through the years.

My mom put my sister and me in an afterschool program called the Bethlehem Community Center. It was a good program for kids in the neighborhood. At the center we would do our homework, get assistance when we needed it, and participate in different activities. My mom put me on the basketball team. I was the only girl on the team. That did not faze me because playing basketball was what I loved to do. In the Bethlehem Center we only had one goal to practice on, but we made the best out of it. Playing on that basketball team with all boys made me tough, aggressive, and a better player. I started playing basketball every day. A lot of girls in the neighborhood did not play basketball, so the boys were my only option to play with. We would play basketball outside on a concrete platform with one goal on each side with the nets torn off the rims. We played basketball through any weather. It was crazy of us, but it was fun.

When I got about 12 years old my mom signed me up for an AAU team called the Lady Bucks. AAU stands for Amateur Athletic Union. AAU is a nonprofit amateur sports organization that is based in the United States. This organization is for the development and promotion of amateur sports and physical fitness programs for children. Playing basketball for that organization gave me the chance to become a better basketball player. It helped me become a better person and a leader, and to improve my skills. There were times when my team traveled to other states to play against other AAU basketball teams. I would go out of town to play basketball in front of college scouts. It was a good opportunity for me so I could see that there were other parts to the world than just Spartanburg. This showed me that there were things around the world that I had not seen yet.

At the age of 14 I was receiving letters from Division I and II colleges. They would write me to let me know that I was a good basketball player and they enjoyed watching me. Some of the colleges that I received letters from were North Carolina Tarheels and Wofford College Terriers. I would play so well that one of the parents who used to come watch me play would call me "Showtime." I gave them a show and good talent to watch. When I played basketball it gave me a way to escape some of the things I was dealing with in my life. It took my mind off of a lot of things. Traveling to play basketball kept me out of the streets of my neighborhood and kept my head on straight. I was playing year round for about seven years straight. I would play from the springtime to the end of the summertime. In the wintertime to springtime I would play for my school. I was kept busy throughout the years, away from some of the crime and drug activity that went on in the neighborhood. The decision my mom made to put me in that organization and any other basketball team I played for had a big impact on my life.

In the previous chapter I mentioned that I have a younger brother. While living in Highland my parents discovered that he was not acting normal like the other toddlers would be acting at his age. He was at the age of 3 and was not talking yet. At that age usually a child is saying a couple of words; he was not saying anything at all. In daycare he was not interacting with the other kids. So, my parents took him to the doctor. They ran some tests on him. The tests came back and he was diagnosed with autism. Autism Spectrum Disorder (ASD) is a serious developmental disorder that impairs the ability to communicate and interact. There were times when he would have seizures. No one in my family knew how to help someone who was having a seizure. The first time he had one we were shaken up and looking for help. The seizure he had came out of nowhere. We stuck together as a family to get him out of his seizures. I felt sorry for my brother because he was diagnosed with that disorder. I felt like it was not fair to him that he was born with that disorder, but we were just fine. I knew the obstacles in life that he would have to go through and face would be tougher for him than it would be for us. He will always have to live with having autism. As the doctors have provided him with medication, he does not have seizures anymore. As my family and his teachers have worked with him closely, he now communicates better and interacts with people more.

A lot of events occurred while I was living in Highland. Some things turned out to be good and some bad. Just because I grew up around negative things and people did not mean that I had to do what they did. The shootings, fights, drug dealings, seeing people go to jail, people on drugs, young people's lives being taken at a young age, and being in the middle of drive-bys made me realize that I did not want to be a part of those things in life. I met a lot of good people that have been taken away from here too soon due to the violence in these streets. There were positive things in Highland also, but many of them were outweighed. The neighborhood made me tough and street smart, and taught me to not give up in life. It does not matter where you come from, it is about where you are going.

CHAPTER 6
SIGHT OF ABUSIVE ACTS

Many years of my childhood I witnessed my mom being abused mentally, physically, verbally, and emotionally. Relationship abuse is a pattern of coercive behaviors used to maintain power and control over a former or current intimate partner. Abuse can be emotional, verbal, mental, financial, sexual, or physical. Abuse has a tendency to escalate over time. When someone uses abuse and violence against a partner it is always part of a larger pattern of control. My parents have been together since the day I was born. Through these years I have seen things that I wish I did not see. As a family we had fun times, but when the bad times came around it had an effect on me. The abusive acts took place in some of the apartment complexes we lived in around

Spartanburg. Most of the abusive acts happened in Highland. My parents argued a lot when I was younger. Those arguments led to physical altercations.

My dad grew up in the same neighborhood that I grew up in, so he experienced a lot of things that I experienced while living in that neighborhood. He grew up seeing abusive relationships in his family. His parents' relationship was on and off. They would have big fights and arguments. After a while they separated from each other. My grandfather moved to North Carolina, leaving my grandmother to raise the kids on her own, so my grandmother raised my father for most of his childhood. My dad and his siblings would visit my grandfather a certain amount of times over the years.

My mom grew up on the west side of Spartanburg. She told me stories about how they lived in poverty. Her parents' relationship did not last long either. My grandparents would have big fights with each other. My mom grew up seeing an abusive relationship as a child also. Both of my parents were witnesses of their parents being in an abusive relationship. This abuse in relationships was passed down to the next generation. The next generation was my parents. They thought what they saw was normal, but it was not. None of those things were right. They saw what their parents went through, so they let the same thing happen in their relationship. There were times when my parents would be arguing in the car while it was in motion. I would be in the backseat then all of a sudden I would see my dad slap her or punch her several times. She would start to cry heavily. Going back to these horrific thoughts still brings some anger to mind, hatred and pain to my heart. There were times when we were at home and they would fight through the house, my dad pushing on her and abusing her. He was way stronger than her, so through much of that she was hopeless. He would control her all the time. I knew when the door was closed when we were at home that they were fighting. I would hear tumbling, cursing, and loud crying. This was all my sister and I saw. We also heard the abusive acts all the time. We would sit together and cry. We knew it was wrong; as bad as we wanted to help her we could not. At the time we were little kids. My mom would call the police on him, kick him out the house, call her father on him, but he still ended up back in her life.

When I got older there were days when I would be so paranoid of the things that were happening around me that I would try to stay around my mom while my dad was around her. I was tired of her being abused over and over. I know I could not stop what was happening, but I was determined to protect my mom some way. If it took me being around her all day so he was not able to abuse her, I would do it. But he did not care if he abused her in front of us. I know that he was not going to try to hurt us in the process of trying to get to her. Seeing my mom being treated that way by my dad hurt me really bad. To see her hurting really hurt me inside. The woman who takes care of me, carried me for nine months, birthed me, and who was always there for me no matter what. I could never accept the abusive acts that were done to her.

The abuse I witnessed growing up as a child made me have resentment, hatred, and anger toward my dad for years after what I saw. My dad and I had arguments a lot of times once I got old enough to speak my mind about the abuse I felt and saw. It made me realize that I did not want to be treated that way and would not treat anyone else that way. I had to learn how to let go of the pain, hatred, and hurt. If I did not it would hold me back in life. I did not realize it was a generational issue that had not been broken until I got older. I would have to be the one to break that generational curse. I had to forgive him for the abuse he caused my mom and me. He did not know any better. Those were the abusive acts he saw when growing up and was a part of as well. It took me a while to forgive him and remove that hatred out of my heart. If your partner is abusing you, you may feel confused, afraid, angry, or trapped. All of those emotions are normal responses to abuse. You may also blame yourself for what is happening.

No matter what others may say, you are never responsible for your partner's actions. So if you are ever in an abusive situation or have been, know that it was a choice for that person to be abusive toward you. Do not take it out on yourself. Take initiative to get out of that relationship; know your self-worth. If you feel like you cannot get out of it, get yourself help and let people you are close with know what is going on.

CHAPTER 7
FREE WILL

———

Free will is the ability to choose between different actions in your life. Everyone is free to choose whatever they want to do in their life. It is up to you to choose what is right or wrong. For most people, the teenage years are when they are influenced by the things they see, what is being played on TV, songs, and other people. They start to imitate things and the people around them. They see people doing the same things other people do, so they feel like they should do it too.

I was the kind of teenager who wanted to be different from other people around me. I had my own way of going about things. I wanted to be a leader and not a follower. People I went to school with and the people who knew me knew that I had my own unique style. I was the type of person who did not like to draw attention to myself. As of today I am still that way. But the way I carried myself stood out to others. By the time I was in the eighth grade I had a lot of admirers. People would walk up to me in school telling me this and that person likes you. They would leave letters in my locker at school. I was not concerned about who the person was, but I would smile about it. I was a shy person at the time, so I really did not say much to people I did not know. I knew a lot of people, but I did not hang with many of them. I continued to play basketball in junior high school and high school in my early teenage years. In the eighth grade I was recruited to play basketball on the lady varsity basketball team for the high school I would be attending in the tenth grade. I know I was only in the eighth grade, but the coach knew that I was a good player, so she recruited me to play on her basketball team. A lot of girls who were on the varsity team did not like it because I was the starting point guard as a freshman. They felt that was unfair to them. I was only doing what my coach recruited me for.

During this time period I was feeling more of an attraction for girls. Someone had approached me one day telling me that a person was interested in me. They told me the person's name and it was a girl. I was not too sure about it at first because I never really talked to girls on a dating type of level. I chose to talk to her. So we started talking on the phone just as friends at first, then being friends led us to deciding to be in a relationship. I was happy being with her. This was my first time actually being in a relationship with someone, so I had no idea how a relationship was supposed to go. All I knew was that it's two people who really like each other, then that like for one another turns into love. But we all know that it does not always go that way. While being in a relationship with that person I kept it a secret and she did too. We used to write letters to each other while we were in school then we would exchange them when we saw one another after school. We would be around each other sometimes, but not very often. She was already in high school when I met her, while I was still in junior high.

I remember my mom was in my room one day messing around in my personal stuff. I was gone somewhere and she found a letter that the girl I was going with wrote me. When I got back home that day she was like, "What is this?" I laugh at it now, but at that moment I was scared. I was shocked that she had found it because I used to hide them in a bag out of sight. So I did not answer her because I did not know what to say. She was like, "You bet not be dating no girls." I lied to her and said she was just a friend. I knew it was not true. I do not think she told my dad about it because he never brought it up to me.

Within 10 months that relationship came to an end. I found out from one of my close friends that she was cheating on me. Then, I actually saw her cheating with someone. While we were going together she was talking and being sexually active with boys. She became pregnant at the time. Everything was hidden from me. We were going to different schools, so I did not know what she had going on at the school she was attending. When my close friend told me what was going on I was heartbroken. This was the first person I thought I was in love with. I invested my time and opened my heart to her. She did not do anything but step on it. When I asked her about it she would continue to lie, but after a few weeks more details came out. The guy she got pregnant by would be down the sidewalk from my apartment visiting his family. That made it even worse and hard for me to not get mad when I would see the guy who was messing with the girl I was supposed to be in love with. Plus she was going to be having a baby by him. In my head I was thinking, *All the things she probably ever told me were a lie.* Some days I would cry and sit in my room alone. This was a new experience for me because I never knew how it felt to have my heart broken. I did not have anyone to talk to about it. I did not go to my parents about it because they did not know that I had been dating a girl. So I had to learn on my own how to get over her and to get to rid of my heartaches. It took me some time but I got over it. After that I moved on. I held a grudge toward her because of the fact that she hurt me real bad.

I know I made the choice to date a girl, but I did not think it would turn out that way. I just wanted to date the gender that I was more attracted to. Most people believe that it is a sin. They believe that for the reason that God made Adam and Eve. I did not really worry about that because I knew that He loves me no matter what gender I chose to be with. Back in those days dating the same sex was a very bad thing to do. I continued to date girls anyway. I would rather not label myself. I have dated a boy and girls. Not having a label attached to my sexual preference gives me the option to not feel boxed in or tied down to a certain title. A label can bring forth negative images and clichés. If you are labeled people expect you to fit in a certain category and act a particular way. My sexual preference does not define me as a person. My free will was being able to live my life and being able to make the decisions that I wanted to make. God gives us the free will. I chose to date girls because I was more attracted to them. I have the free will to be who I want to be and do what I want to do. Now that I am older I understand that God has His will for me also.

CHAPTER 8
REOCCURRING PAIN

After having my first experience of being in a relationship I did not give up on being in them. I continued to be in more relationships. I was in the kind of relationships that would only last from six to ten months. Most of the relationships I was in consisted of cheating, lying, arguments, insecurities, selfishness, being used for one's needs, anger, and betrayal. The relationships I was in or people I dated were not all based on bad things happening. I also had good times with a few of them. In some of the relationships that I was in the girls I dated were looking for me to be masculine, but I was more feminine. The only thing about me was that my appearance had a more masculine look to it. That made them think I was hardcore. They wanted me to be a certain way.

I have always been the kind of person who would never cheat in a relationship. When I chose to be with someone I stuck by my word and did things the way I knew how. I never wanted to hurt anyone, but if I did it was unintentionally. Most of the time I was the one being hurt. I was the loyal, genuine, caring, sensitive, and faithful kind of person in most of my relationships. I am not perfect because I know I made mistakes too. I remember being one-sided, not considering other people's feelings. I could be a very mean, stubborn, and stern person at times. The softer side of me had been suppressed from when I was growing up. From getting whoopings I experienced pain and hurt at an early age. I carried pain and anger within my heart to most of those relationships. I would try to show this tougher side. That was not really me. I was the one with the huge heart. Most times I covered it up to protect myself from continuing to be hurt by people. When I would uncover it is when I fell in love with someone, then my heart would get crushed. My trust issues would build up after every relationship ended badly. It was obvious that something was wrong in the relationships I was choosing to be in. It was a cycle of them lasting for a few months then ending.

The Chosen One

I had graduated high school and gotten a scholarship to go to a college in Spartanburg. I was in a period of my life where I was tired of hiding my sexuality. I only cared about my parents knowing. I was not concerned about other people knowing. I was 18 when I got to college. I felt like I was a young adult now, so if my parents did not accept my sexuality I would continue to do what I wanted to do. I figured at that point that they did not have a say-so. I did not want my sexuality to be a secret anymore, especially from my parents. I wrote them a letter when I was working at my summer job. In the letter I came out to them about my sexuality, how long it had been going on, and that I did not want to be judged. After my mom read it she probably mentioned it to my dad, but she would usually be the one to speak for the both of them. She told me that she already knew and that she was just waiting for me to tell her about it when I got ready. She told me that she accepts me for who I am and what I wanted to do. She let me know that what I told her was not going to change the fact that I am her daughter. I was going to be her child regardless of my sexuality. My parents are not against people who are gay. I have two of the coolest parents. When they both accepted me I felt so relieved. A big load had been lifted off of me. I was very happy after that.

The first year I was in college I played basketball. I was on basketball and academic scholarships. I was a great student-athlete. Everything for me was going well at the time. In my offseason for basketball I had workouts. I would play pickup basketball with my teammates. One day when I was playing basketball with my teammates things took a turn for the worst. Someone threw me a pass down the basketball court while I was on a fast break. I was all the way down the court while everyone else was far behind me trying to catch up to me. When I got the ball I did a left-hand layup. I landed on my left knee like I would normally, but this time when I went to make the layup my kneecap shifted out of place, then it shifted back in place on its own. It happened so fast, but I remember seeing it happen. The pain was so bad, it was the worst pain I had ever felt with an injury. The day it happened the doctor that my college sent athletes to was not around. He was on vacation and would not be back in town for a couple of days. So the trainer gave me some medication for the pain like Aleve. I took the medication, but nothing was strong enough to block that pain I was having. A few hours after going back to my dorm room with help from my teammates the pain got even worse. There was nothing the trainer could do, the doctor was not in town.

When I got to my dorm room I got dizzy and light-headed. At one point I tried to go to the restroom.

I had a long, black brace around my leg to keep it straight. When I tried to stand up on one leg with my crutches with pain shooting up my leg, I started to have a panic attack. My vision got blurry, my breathing was shortening, I could not hear anything, and everything looked like it was closing in. I was gasping for oxygen, trying to see and hear things. It lasted for about 10 minutes. I thought I was about to die. Luckily my roommate was there to help me sit back down, then the panic attack stopped. I know the panic attack came from me being overwhelmed with the pain and my injury. All I could do was cry and sit. There was so much going through my mind at the time. So the woman over our dorm room called my parents to pick me up. I wanted to go home; there was no way I could stay there at the time. I wanted to see a doctor the same day. My parents took me to the hospital. The hospital gave me some pain relievers to ease the pain. Then, they referred me to a specialist for the next day.

I went to the doctor, and he did X-rays and saw what happened to my knee. He told me that I had a left knee dislocation. My ligaments had stretched too far also. He said that I would not need surgery just physical therapy. So I went to physical therapy. I went back to play basketball when they released me from physical therapy. My knee was still not fixed and I continued to have pain in it, so I went back to the doctor. He told me that I needed to get an arthroscopic knee surgery. I was broken and devastated. He did not catch this problem from the start. That surgery was going to take me out for a while. My mom had to come up with money to pay for the surgery because my Medicaid got cut off a few weeks before my injury happened. Things were not looking too good for me at that moment. My mom got some of the money some way for me to have surgery; she scraped up everything she had so that I could get it done. She did not have help at the time from my father because he was in and out of jobs. I had to get a care credit card for the rest of the amount that she was not able to pay. That credit card put more debt on me, but I badly needed the surgery.

When we got all of that out of the way I got to get my knee surgery. The surgery took four hours. I received a screw in my kneecap to hold it together while it was healing, and they reconstructed my patella and worked on my ligaments. It was so much at one time. I was so down, overwhelmed, lost, depressed, and unsure whether I would be able to play again. I went through therapy again. This time I had to learn how to walk again and work my way up from there. All of this stuff that I was going through was shocking for me. My body started to change, as well as the way I viewed myself. I had gained 20 pounds and was not the person I used to be.

The Chosen One

At the time I was going with this girl, off and on. She would not be around or help me out as much. She did not want to be with someone who was sitting in the house a lot on crutches and who had gained weight. She felt like I could not do anything for her. I was going through a lot at the time in my life, but the way she was treating me showed me that she did not care. It was only making things worse. That relationship came to an end. It came out that she was cheating on me and had lied about everything. One time she lied to me about being pregnant — it was her way of ending things with me. She went on to tell me that she went to the doctor and had an abortion. After everything finally ended with us she said that she was never pregnant or had an abortion. She went through the measures of telling me she had stomach pains and that she had to take certain kinds of medicine to flush things out from the abortion. This was crazy how she would make up a lie like this just to get me out of her life or hurt me. My heart was broken from the breakup, the lies, cheating, and my injury at the same time.

Playing basketball was my first love. I felt like I had lost that. I went to go play again after I completed physical therapy, but my knee was still in pain. Something just did not feel right. I went back to the doctor for the third time to get an X-ray. This time he said it was a piece of cartilage sticking out causing me pain, and it could have been the screw that was in my kneecap. So I had surgery again to have the cartilage, arthritis, and metal screw removed from my kneecap. I completed therapy again. A few months later I was back to playing basketball. I had graduated from the college I went to in Spartanburg then transferred to a four-year college in South Carolina. They were not offering me a scholarship, so I took the chance to walk on. I was very thankful to be able to play basketball again. I tried to play one more year in college, but I ended up just helping the team out on the side. That was the end of my career. I did not want to feel like I was giving up on my passion. I just needed more time to get adjusted to the way my knee was functioning now. I really wanted to continue playing basketball, but my knee was not ready. That is where my heart was and will always be. I made the decision to focus on my education more and graduate with a bachelor's degree.

In my senior year of college I took classes online and worked part time at a plant. I met a woman through Facebook. We had known each other from living in the same neighborhood that I grew up in. We crossed paths a few years later and through Facebook, she was telling me that she was interested in me. I was not too sure about talking to her at first. She was like five years older than me, had kids, dropped out of school at an early age so that she could take care of her kids, and just had gotten out of jail a year before for some drug charges. At that time I had just gotten out of a relationship a few months before meeting her. I thought I was over that past relationship, but I really was not. I did not give myself time to heal from my past relationships, so I was still walking around with a broken heart.

When that woman came along we started talking. I was desperate and felt like I needed to be with someone. You can say that I was vulnerable. I wanted to be wanted. I wanted to be approved of and loved. I was trying to fill a void that I had in me in so many relationships. I was not looking within myself to fill the void. I was looking for other people to do it and that is where I would fall short. I thought I could leave one person then get in another relationship or date someone so that I could get over my previous one. Later I found out that does not do anything but make things worse. She and I continued to talk anyway. We started to get closer overtime. I learned stuff about her and what she went through growing up. She had dealt with a lot of things in life. One day she told me that she was married, but her husband was in jail for drug charges. She told me that he had to do eight years. She told me about how they went to jail around the same time and told me about their marriage. She let me know that she was not happy with the position she was at in her life. I accepted her, her past, and her kids. I did not pass any judgment toward her. She mentioned a lot of things to me throughout the time period we were talking, but there was a lot that I would find out later that she lied about. We continued to talk, but never committed to being in a relationship together due to the fact that she was married. I started to fall for her and she said that she felt the same about me.

Once my heart got involved things took a turn for the worse. I thought she had changed into someone who I did not know, but all along she was that same person. Her true colors started to show. I invested my heart, money, and time into her. I put her needs before mine including her kids' needs. I helped her out a lot financially; she never had my back. It was a time when I was without a job. Before I was jobless I was working at a plant job for four years on and off for summer help. They did not have an open position for me so that I could continue to work there year around. This was the same year I had graduated from college. So I went without a job for a few months. It was hard trying to find a job at the time, I did not have any experience in my major that I went to school for. No one was trying to hire me. I was basically broke and was still supporting her at times with the small amount of money I had saved up. When I would ask her if I could borrow some money from her she would tell me she did not have it. She had money to gamble with and would win. Not one time did she ask if I needed anything. I was there for her 99% of the time. When I needed her just that one time, she was not there for me.

Once my feelings got deeper for her I felt like I was stuck. I had a connection with her that I did not have with the people in my past. I thought I was in love. I could not tell if she really loved me though. Maybe she had a strong like for me. When I started to have this deep love for her I became blind to the way she was treating me, so I put up with it. I would use money to try to keep her around so that I could receive love. I was afraid of being alone, not knowing that money could not buy love. I was trying to buy her love, but the love was not even there anyway. I had a lot to learn. In my mind I was thinking, *This is the person for me, this is who I want to be with.* I guess that is how most people think when they are in love with someone.

I wanted to be in a relationship with her. When I brought it up she would say she did not want to talk about that. One day I brought it up again and she was like, let me get myself together, then we can go from there. So I waited for her to get herself together. The thing about it is she was never trying to get herself together. She had me on hold while she was having relations with other people. She left me thinking we would have been together, but we were not going to be. Anything she wanted me to do I would do it. She knew what kind of person I was. I was a helpful and caring person. Even though we were not going together I was doing things that even couples don't do for their partner. That is how bad it was. I would even think of ways that she could have a better life. I would share my ideas with her. For example, I was going to help her get her GED because before she could finish getting her GED they released her from jail. She really did not like that; she thought I was talking down on her. I was only seeing ways where she could improve her life for the sake of her kids and herself in the long run. I saw ways that she could better herself; she could not see those ways. She would tell me that I think I am better than other people. That was never my intention. When I look at people I see opportunities within for them to better themselves. I care that they have a better life — especially if they're unhappy; maybe that is a cry for help. The difference between us is that she was not awakened. She resisted change; I was all about changing. I had to learn that I cannot help everyone, but I can try to get them to understand what I am saying. Once I try and they resist that is my signal to stop trying. You cannot save someone who does not want to be saved, and that was her.

She would talk down on me and pick on the way I was as a person. Those words would play over and over in my head to the point that I believed them about myself. That would hurt my feelings, but she did not care. If I would bring it up to her she did not want to hear it. When I was around her at times if I would smile and be happy for no reason she would get mad about it. She would ask me why I was smiling. It was like she did not want me to be happy because she was not, so I would try to have a serious face around her. I could not be myself around her without her being mad. The positive energy I did have in me before I met her was sucked out of me by her negative energy and words. If I was not talking about money and ways to benefit her she did not want to hear it. When I was around her she would be texting and talking to other people like I was not around at all. She had no respect for me. We would get into big arguments, stop talking, and I would give in. I wanted to cut things completely off plenty of times, but I would always go back. She was like my drug, something that I had to have. I was only being her doormat really. There were no boundaries set, so it was like I tolerated everything that was being done to me. It went on for about two years off and on until I finally let go. She was the kind of person who knew the game and I did not have a clue about it. It was played on her plenty of times, now she was using it on me. She did not want to change her ways, so my ways were changing for the worse. I was changing into someone else: It was who she wanted me to be. If I would tell her no when she wanted something she would get mad and ignore me. She told me if she could not get it from me, she could get it from somewhere else.

There were times when she would brag to people, telling them how I would do stuff for her, and call me stupid. I know that was true for sure because people would come back to tell me about it. While I was supporting her she had other people on the side. She was probably treating them the same way as she was treating me. That made me look stupid around town to the people who knew what was going on. My friends and people who knew me heard that I was talking to her. They would ask me why I was talking to her and tell me, "She is not your type" or "She is not the one for you." They would tell me that they could see me with a classier person or someone who had something going for herself. They knew we were on different levels, but I was just not seeing it that way. I was picturing her as a good person. She fooled me with her smile, seeming innocent, and being a cool, laid-back person. I had to realize that everything that glitters is not gold. Just because of the way she was when I first met her did not mean she could not have been a person who would play with someone's heart. Looks do not mean anything if that person is damaged on the inside.

She never wanted to take trips with me; she would make up excuses to not go. We probably went out with each other two times. After a while I would be the one calling and texting her first. At the beginning it was the other way around, but things shifted. If she reached out to me it was only because she wanted something from me. I would see other people driving her car around town, not knowing she was having relations with them too. When I asked her about it she would ignore me, or tell me we do not go together or that I was crazy. I was not crazy — I saw a lot of things with my own eyes. I had the impression that she would have the kind of heart I had, but I have learned that everyone will not have the kind of heart that I have.

When I was going through these things with her on and off I was changing. I realized that she did not want me. I knew by her actions and the way she treated me. My issue was that I did not know how to let go. I started staying in my room all the time, not eating, losing weight, and crying all the time. I became depressed, stressed, mean, hopeless, bitter, and negative. I was brought all the way down to the point where I did not want to be on earth anymore. I did not want to live life anymore if I had to continue to go through so much pain. I felt alone and unloved. I filled my head with thoughts that degraded me as a person. My closest female friends stuck by my side at this time and gave me advice. I kept asking myself,

Why me, why can't I get it right? I had no choice but try to move on with my life. I met other girls who came along after that, but it seemed like they were not up to no good either. I continued meeting heartless, damaged, and hurt people. I was meeting those kinds of girls because that is who I was on the inside. I was attracting those kinds of people in my life. I would try to give them the benefit of the doubt, but that was when their true colors showed. I started thinking, *Maybe it is not my time right now to have relations with someone.* My mind was still on that woman, and that is where my heart was.

All the stuff I saw and went through with her broke my heart completely into pieces. It really hurt me to my soul. I was deceived and betrayed by her many times. I had gone from relationship to relationship without healing, only carrying all that pain. Pain was even built up from what I saw as a child in my household, getting whoopings, and my knee injury. I had gone through pain physically, mentally, verbally, financially, and emotionally. When I got with that woman it got worse than it ever was. All that pain I held in my heart had broken me down. I could not bear all that pain anymore. I had reached my boiling point. There were times I would cry so much that I could feel that something inside of me was hurting — it was my heart. I was giving up on life. I had stopped believing in love. It was so bad I did not even want to hear or see the world. I would stop listening to love songs. I definitely did not want to hear the word "love." I had grudges toward all the people who had hurt me in some way. I blamed love because I felt like it hurt me too. I have learned now that love was not to blame. The hurt came from the people I was with or the situations I was in. I was living with a dark cloud above me, with Lucifer around me. I know we are not supposed to question God's work, but I was at that time. I wanted to know my purpose here on earth and why I was created. Later God would show me the answers to my questions.

CHAPTER 9
SPIRITUAL AWAKENING (PIVOTAL POINT)

―✥✥―

All that pain I had endured and held over the years was finally catching up with me. I never took the time out to heal from any of the things that hurt me. It was taking a toll on my mind, body, soul, and life. The last person that I had relations with I could not seem to let go. The more I wanted to be in her life, the more lessons I was being taught. I knew that I was supposed to have ended it long ago. Since I did not leave the previous times I said I was going to leave, I continued to stick around and ended up hurting myself. As I continued to put up with her I would get fed up more and more to the point where I was so torn. I finally said to myself that it was time for a change.

In the process of cutting her out of my life I started searching for answers. I was very lost in my mind and this world. I was questioning my sexual preference and other things about my life. I turned bitter, mean, and cold-hearted. I was drinking, smoking tobacco products, and partying more to get my mind off of things. Everybody who knows me knows that I am not a drinker or smoker. I am usually the sober one. I was hanging with people and crowds that I usually would not be with. I was trying to find my place but it was not in any of those places where I was trying to search. My heart was filled with fear. That fear was hindering my heart. I did not have any confidence, self-esteem, courage, identity, faith, positive energy, and other traits that were important for someone to have. For example, I felt like my identity was stripped from me because I put all of myself in her. I had stopped taking care of myself and was tending to her needs. I was worried about her so much I did not even know myself anymore. While searching for answers desperately I even went to a psychic a couple of times. I was afraid to go because I had never been before. I wanted to test the waters, as some people would say, basically to see if it was real. I went to her and she told me that the girl I had relations with was my soul mate. She also was telling me that the girl loved me and we would be together one day. As open as I was, I was sitting there believing most of it. I was not listening to my intuition. At the time all I wanted to hear her say was that the girl loved me. I took that statement and ran with it. It boosted my ego up, not realizing that it was untrue. Then in my mind I was like, *That girl's actions do not add up with what the psychic is telling me, so something has to be wrong.*

There was a fee for going to visit the psychic, and that added up overtime. So I stopped going to her and saved my money. I started to believe that the woman was not telling the truth. I would ask myself, *Why can't I just let go of my past with that girl and stop causing myself all this pain?* Now I realize that I had a soul tie with her. A soul tie is like a linkage in the realm of two people. It links their souls together, which can bring forth either beneficial or negative results. Soul ties can be formed from having sex outside of marriage. We had several sexual encounters. It felt like I was tied to her, but she had no tie with me. She was free and I was not. At that moment I did not know anything about a soul tie. Now, when I think about it the symptoms I had when I was trying to end things with her matched the description of a soul tie.

Some of the symptoms are obsessive preoccupation with another person, tendencies to be passive, inability to truly forgive from the heart, hearing another person's voice playing over and over in the mind, and fear of speaking the truth to another person. For example, I was afraid of speaking the truth to her after being shutdown several times for sharing my insights on ways she could better her life and not be so stressed. So I stopped being myself for the sake of what she did not like. I had tendencies to be passive with her. When she wanted something done or needed me for something I would not say no. I would always say yes most of the time. The soul tie I had with her had a bad affect on me. I learned about the soul tie when I moved on with my life. Once I got the soul tie broken by the grace of God, I tried to get back out there in the dating world. I just have not been able to come across someone who is for me. I kept meeting girls that were liars, confused, heartless, against love, not mature enough for me, or had nothing going for themselves. I was not interested in those kinds of girls. I wanted something real, not fake.

While I was still lost and still trying to find myself in this world I had an experience that opened my eyes. This is the experience that would change my life forever. One night I was working third shift in the summertime at a plant job. I just had gotten back from a vacation with my family earlier that day. That night all of a sudden I was not feeling too well. I was at work taping up a box and all of a sudden I got lightheaded. My body got hot, forehead was cold, and my vision got blurry. I got dizzy, started to get a headache, and was sweating, nauseated, and weak. I felt like I was about to pass out. I was fine before I got to work. So I told my manager and she let me go home that night. That next morning I was fine. I did not know what had come over me, but I felt a little different. From that day I started changing in a way I could not explain clearly.

I was changing physically, emotionally, mentally, and spiritually. But I did not know that at the time. I thought it was just a phase of getting over that girl. Physically my hands would tingle, my weight changed and eating habits changed. I noticed aches and pains in my body, feelings of vibration going through my body, dizzy spells, and night sweats. Sometimes I would wake up in the middle of the night with my body and clothes dripping in water. I was feeling tired a lot, my energy level was going up and down, and my sleeping patterns changed with sleepless nights. I would toss and turn throughout the nights not getting enough rest. Emotionally I wanted to withdraw from my family and friends. I did not want to mingle and talk to anyone. I felt like I was going through a transition and needed to be alone. I just felt like a mess and did not want to be seen that way. Mentally I felt like I was losing my mind and was losing control. My thoughts were all over the place thinking about the next steps I was going to take in life. Spiritually my dreams started being more vivid and intense. I would have dreams that showed me signs about my waking life and the people in it. I was empathetic and sensitive toward other people's feelings, had an urge to find out my life purpose, and many other symptoms. For example, I did not know my path in life, so I started to have the urge to question life. I wanted to know what my life purpose was because I was lost. I wanted to live a more meaningful life.

I made the decision that it was time to change. I was stagnant for too long. I was open to God's work. Before that when I was the old me I was afraid of God. I had the fear of not knowing what was bigger than me. Fear had taken over my body and heart — it was only Satan trying to take over me. I was close-minded, not knowing that God was my number one supporter and healer. My relationship with God was what my life was missing. I started praying to God every day. He started showing me things and bringing guidance into my life. God was there with me all along. The experience that I explained to you that I went through was a Spiritual Awakening. A spiritual awakening is a shift in consciousness, an apperception of reality which had been previously unrealized. A spiritual awakening is felt throughout one's body, heart, mind, and soul. My body was being awakened from the inside and outside. My chakras were being opened also. Chakras are energy centers within the human body that help to regulate all its processes from organ function to the immune system and emotions. All the symptoms I mentioned that happened to me tie in with the spiritual awakening and chakras.

As I continued to go through the process of a spiritual awakening God was there and guided me through it. This was something that I would not have been able to get through on my own. My body was being stripped from the identity I had. I was going through a cleansing process inside and out. All the toxic emotions and negative energy were being cleansed from my body. I mentioned the things I was experiencing to some of my close friends. None of them believed me; they thought I was weird and going crazy. I do not think any of them have ever had that experience before. They did not understand me at all. There was a big difference between us. I was being awakened, when they had not reached that point in their lives yet. After that I kept it a secret because no one understood me. I was misunderstood most of my life by the people around me, so this was not my first time experiencing misunderstandings.

I have always felt like I was different from others, but I did not know exactly what it was. Through this process I noticed that my mind was opening up more. God and the angels were guiding me even more toward the things that would help me build a new me.

There used to be days that I would wake up and the television would be on the OWN channel. The owner of that television station is Oprah Winfrey. Most people know who she is. She has played in many great movies and has had *The Oprah Winfrey Show* for years. On Sunday morning I would watch *Super Soul Sunday*. On that show she interviewed different people who wrote books and shared experiences that happened in their lives. The first person I watched on the show was Gary Zukav. He is an author of many great books. The book they were talking about on the show was called *The Seat of the Soul*. The book was about all the aspects of life, especially the soul. The main thing I remember from the book was being able to separate the ego from who you are supposed to be. He talked about aligning with your higher self to become your authentic self. I felt like Gary Zukav was talking to me. At the moment I was experiencing a spiritual breakthrough, which was the only way to connect to my higher self and experience a truly authentic life. I knew it was time for a change; I was not happy.

From that point on I continued to watch Oprah's television show. I started to have dreams of things I never had before. I researched articles online so that I could gain more knowledge about life and the things I needed to know. I would read more books, particularly in the self-help section. When I felt like I needed improvement in certain areas of my life I would go to Barnes and Noble to pick out books to read. I would meet people at my jobs who I was able to share my experience with and gain knowledge from. God was showing me all kinds of signs and leading me. My journey of building a new me was just beginning.

My outlook on life changed. I saw things differently. I was still going through my healing process. I took the initiative to apologize to people I may have hurt in my past or present. I asked if they could forgive me. If they felt like they could not forgive me, I would forgive them anyway. Then, I went through the process of forgiving myself. I had to forgive myself also to release the resentment, hatred, and grudges, and to get my power back. If I did not forgive myself the people I had bitterness, hatred, or resentment toward would still have power over me. It was like they had control over me when I held something against them. So I had to get my power back and release the toxic emotions in order for my heart to be free. I stopped being so hard on myself for the mistakes I made. At those times I was very young and still learning. What I know now I did not know then. I was not taught certain things about relationships and what to expect in them. I did not have those conversations with my parents like some people did. I forgive people because some people don't know any better. They might not know the right way to treat someone if they have been treated badly their whole life. We are raised different ways, taught things a certain way, and go through different things in life. Most of those people who hurt others are hurt themselves. They don't realize it, so forgive them for not knowing any better. We are all going through a living and learning process.

While continuing to be transformed I notice more things that were changing about me. I started to separate myself from others for short periods at a time. I needed to elevate myself. Distractions are everywhere, so I needed to escape them. I got off of social media. At one point I let my cell phone get turned off. The things I was once interested in did not serve me as much anymore. I was focused on becoming a better person and connecting to my inner self. My belief system was changing: I wanted more freedom and less material things. I was more drawn to personal development, had a deep desire to connect with nature more, and had a desire to eat healthier and take better care of my body. For example, I was more interested in finding things out about myself that I could work on, so that I could grow. I started embracing my strengths and weaknesses instead of looking down upon myself. God created me a certain way for particular reasons. All I needed to do was love myself first, then everything else would come.

CHAPTER 10
GOD'S WORK

I went on in life seeing things through an awakened eyesight and mind. Things continued to get better. The journey I was taking helped me learn myself even more. I learned a lot of lessons from what I had been through. I know I will continue to learn more lessons as life goes on. The lessons I learned helped me change and grow. Some of the biggest lessons I have learned so far are to forgive myself and others and to not try to control things in life; just let go and let God deal with it. When I practiced and lived by those things a lot of dead weight was lifted off of me.

I knew that God was still working on me. I was always ready for a change. I work two jobs; one is for a cleaning service as a part-time employee. I am a janitor for an insurance company at that job. I was blessed to get that job; it has helped me earn more money so that I can pay my student loans on time. I am in debt behind student loans for thousands of dollars, so I have to take the responsibility to pay them back some way. The thought of being in debt puts a strain on me. I am pretty sure people with student loans feel the same way I feel. Every month I try my best to pay the debt collectors on top of the other bills I have to pay.

My position at my full-time job is a Support Systems Analyst I. I work in the Customer Care center. A few months after I started that job I met a lady. She was a nice, smart, outgoing, good, and cool person. She asked me through instant messaging how I was doing. I replied, "I'm doing fine." She told me she noticed that I am reserved and stay to myself most of the time. I agreed with her. She started explaining to me who I was as a person, what I was dealing with at the time, the pain I had been through, and many other things she would not have known. But she described me like no other person could. She was reading me — it was creepy at first. Then, a few days later she said, "God sent me here to help you." I was so shocked that I did not know what to say. I paused with my jaw dropped and a surprised look on my face. To know that God was there for me since day one made me very happy. She told me that she was waiting on me to come forth. I was sitting at my desk telling myself *this is so amazing*, with a big smile on my face. None of this is made up; all of it is real. We went on for days talking about life, God, angels, our lives, building myself, goals, and anything I felt curious about. I never met anyone in my life like her. She spoke life into me. Before I met her I learned a lot on my own and with the guidance of God. Listening to her made the pieces come together. I have had a lot of *aha* moments, as Oprah Winfrey would say on her television show, thinking this is why that happened and why I have felt this way.

The lady understood that I have been underestimated my whole life. No one has really known my abilities until I have proven them wrong. I was the one who was in the background of any activity or anything I participated in. I was looked over a lot; it was like I was not noticed. The thing about it is I was actually the leader all this time, but I never stepped up to the plate. I would seem like a follower, but I was not created to follow. I was created to be a leader. The knowledge people thought they had, I was already gifted with it before they knew the information. I just did not show my presence and wisdom. My confidence was not where it was supposed to be at that time. God used the lady I met at work to reach out to me so that I could continue to learn, grow, and show myself to the world. The creator of a lot of great movies, Tyler Perry, once said, "Sometimes you're supposed to be hidden. It's not your time to be seen yet. At the right time God will reveal you, your talents, and everything you've done to the world. But in the meantime prepare." Those words touched me because I felt like he was talking to me. That made me more open to changing and expanding.

When I continued to get hurt in most of my relationships I gave up on love. I put it in my mind that love is not for me. People would say, "Love will find you, but only if you are not looking for it." Even though I gave up on love, in my mind and heart I had this intense urge for it. I wanted to give love also. It was something I could not cover up. As people we are created to love. God is love, He created love, and love conquers all. Love is the greatest gift of all gifts. God's love is everlasting and unconditional. I was trying to fight the urge and play tough, but my soul was calling for it. I continued to work on myself, read articles, and research things about life. I discovered that the one thing I was resisting was what I actually needed. That one important thing was love. I questioned myself about love plenty of times — *how am I not getting love right?* Now I know the answer to that. I did not know what love was, I was not loving myself first, did not know how to love or relate to others, and I was filled with fears from my past love experiences. I only knew love by what I saw growing up from my parents being together, movies, other people's relationships, and songs. If I was in a relationship with someone and I liked them a whole lot I thought that could have been love. But now I know it was not love. Most of my relationships were about lust. Lust is a physical emotion and reaction to someone else's physical appearance. Lust does not last long and is more about immediate gratification. Real love is everlasting, while lust runs out over a short period of time.

Growing up I did not know how love was supposed to feel. My parents or family members never talked about love with me. If it was something about feelings in our household, it was not discussed. I grew up not knowing how to express my feelings. My feelings were suppressed since I was a child. Most people assume they know what love is, but they really do not. When I realized that about myself I took the opportunity to learn love and to love differently from the way I was loving. I do not blame my parents because they never taught me certain things in life that were important. They were most likely not taught certain things either while growing up. This was a generational issue that was passed down from generation to generation. I had to forgive them. I forgave myself also for not knowing what I did not know before I started to learn things over. I forgave my parents, the people who hurt me, and myself. Then a burden was lifted off of me. My heart was not so heavy anymore. I did not feel like I had to continue to blame anyone for my pain. There was no one to blame, and that is where forgiveness took place. My heart was still undergoing a healing process. I knew that this would be a new start for me. I stopped looking for love; instead I started to become love. I had to learn how to love myself first, so that other things could fall into place within my life.

As I progress sometimes I look back on how far I came in my life. It is a blessing to be where I am today. I truly believe I am blessed. I feel like I am the chosen one. God has chosen me to go through the spiritual awakening, connect to my higher self, and be a servant to Him. Many people do not get to experience what I have experienced, so many people are only willing to touch the surface levels of life. They are afraid to be awakened to the truth, staying limited to only what they know rather than what they are capable of. Being trapped in a state of fear and ego will get you nowhere if you desire to connect to your higher self. The moment I put that together is when I told myself I was chosen for a reason. When I realized that I felt chills go through my body. I knew right then that I was someone special. My whole life people have tried to change me in a way that would satisfy them. People would share their opinions about me to try to get me to change. I was known to be different. My personality stood out to other people. Different does not mean that a person needs to be changed; it might just be that they were created to be that way. Being different can be good.

Over the years people's opinions had gotten to me until I looked back on who I used to be before I let the opinions change me. I went back to that place to embrace my strengths and weaknesses. The things that people would pick on me about, I would look at those things as a gift and not a curse. I accepted everything about me. But if something needed to be changed about me I would see if it was affecting me as a person, then work on that particular thing. If it was not affecting me I would just accept it as a part of me. One of the things I had to come to terms with about myself was to be honest and true to myself. When I did that my true self was rediscovered. When you are true to yourself you are being yourself. You are not trying to be someone you idolize, someone you see on television, or your friends. You become the authentic you. I can say that I am a true, authentic, special, and original person. My spiritual awakening experience changed my life tremendously.

When I was awakened, I recognized some of the things I was gifted with. The traits I figured were my weaknesses were really my gifts. I could actually use them to help people in the world and to make the world a better place. For instance, being very sensitive could be someone's strength or weakness trait. I thought being sensitive was a bad thing growing up because people would always pick on me about being too sensitive. People would get over on me because I was overly sensitive. After I embraced that trait about myself I felt like some people are not blessed with the sensitivity level that I have. Instead of looking at it as a weakness it became one of my strengths. We need more sensitive and compassionate people in the world today. Sensitive people love and think deeply about life. Some are loyal, honest, and true. The simple things sometimes mean the most to them. They do not need to change or harden themselves. Their purity makes them who they are. Those things let me know that I was blessed with this trait for a reason.

Some of my other gifts are that I am good at helping people, I care about others, and I am observant of people/things around me. I know that I have the intuitive ability to instantly empathize with people. I know how to comfort them. For example, I am able to listen to someone's situation and instantly have a connection to how they are feeling. People who do not know me open up to me willingly about their life without me asking them to. At times I have the ability to soak up the moods and energies of the people around me. Sometimes I would not even notice that I had soaked up someone else's energy; it can easily rub off on me. Feeling other people's energy can be draining, especially if the energy is negative. For example, I may be around someone who is having a bad day; the next minute I may begin to have these negative emotions. The negative emotions from that person have rubbed off on me. I feel more than what other people may feel a lot of times. There were times when I was a child, around age 10, where I would be in church with my family members and I would get emotional from the other people who were emotional around me. I did not know at the time that I was empathetic. Sometimes I would go to church and people's energy would be overwhelming for me. I did not know what to do. That was a sign God was giving me, but I was too young to notice.

Precognitive abilities also play a role in my life. You may be wondering what that means; It is the ability to have foreknowledge of an event. All those gifts I mentioned to you about me were not acknowledged until I became more spiritually awakened to myself and the world around me. In my heart, mind, and soul I know that God is using me to bless others. I have come to understand on my journey that everyone has a purpose here on earth. Purpose is something you were born to do in the world. Your purpose will usually be connected to a gift that you were born with. You use your gift then it gives you a platform. With that platform you effect change in the world. By effecting change in the world that is what your purpose is. You use your gift to make the world a better place. With the opportunity to connect to my higher self I not only listened to what it is in my heart to do in life, but I listened to my soul also. That is called a soul's purpose. A soul purpose is the calling from your soul to let you know that your purpose needs to be pursued in order for you to be satisfied with your life. Once the soul continues to be satisfied you will truly experience more happiness and joy. I have not reached that point yet, but I have faith that I am on my way.

At times an urge comes over me: It is the urge to pursue my soul's purpose. My purpose is what I am supposed to be truly pursuing here on earth. I feel like my soul is calling me to support others through teaching, coaching, healing, or love. The gifts that I know I have tie in with my life purpose. I believe some of the actions that will have to be taken in order for me to fully pursue my life purpose are to totally love my fellow human beings, and understand how the universe functions and how people function. I would have to learn how to nurture key relationships, fully develop and apply my intuition, think lovingly, and compassionately work with people. When I am at work I have a feeling within me that the jobs I am at right now are not my purpose, so I feel like I am unsatisfied most of the time. But I know that God takes us through certain tasks in life so that we can learn and grow from them. I am thankful to have two jobs. I believe that everything happens for a reason. I am at my jobs for a number of reasons. I look at it as a steppingstone. God is trying to get me to adapt to the environment I am in and the things I deal with daily. I am being prepared for something much bigger that has yet to come. Once my task has been completed at these jobs He will move me to another one that will prepare me for the job of my dreams. Having patience plays a big part in this and every part of my life. People have always said, "Patience is a virtue, good things come to those who wait." When it is time God will direct you. God has chosen me to be on this particular path. I am just a student in His class, eager to learn.

CHAPTER 11
BUILDING AND ADJUSTING

I used my strength to get past the hard times I have been through in my life. I kept my determination to get through the tough times. If I ever reached a point where I thought about giving up, God was there to give me the strength to carry on. You never know what you are capable of until you are faced with a challenge. Some way you find a way to get through it. You never know how strong you are until you are tested. There is a saying, "Anything that does not kill you will make you stronger." That statement is true because I am living proof of it. The more tests you get through the stronger you become. My strength has gotten me through a lot in my life. I figure giving up would be too easy, so I continue to keep pushing myself to become better.

In this continuous process of becoming my authentic self I am continuing to build myself and grow into the person God intended me to be. A few tasks I do so that I can continue to build myself are setting goals, meditating, and listening to motivational speakers. For example, when I set goals I write down how I will accomplish them and hold myself accountable to get them accomplished. Setting goals for myself helps me acknowledge the things I want in life, so that I can grow as a person. As I continue to use those things in my life. I have started to become peaceful within, inspired, creative, and ambitious, and I follow my inner guidance. For example, when I meditate I am able to relax my body and mind. By doing that I feel more happy and peaceful within.

I lived most of my life in the past or future. Living that way took away from what was happening at the moment in my life. I was not living in the present. When I became more aware I started to be mindful. Instead of life passing me by I live in the moment now and am awakened to experience. I am able to observe myself and my thoughts more closely. Being honest with myself and the people around me has taken me a long way also. When I am honest with myself I can be myself and not pretend to be something I am not.

The Chosen One

One day I realized that the way I was thinking had to be changed if I wanted to build myself up more from where I had started. I have experienced being at my lowest point in my life, so I do not want to jeopardize how hard I have worked to get to where I am today. I am not trying to go backward, so I choose to continue going forward. One day I was watching a video on YouTube of an episode from the Steve Harvey talk show. He was saying, "If you want the secret to living a happy life read this book." The book was called *The Secret*. The author of the self-help book is Rhonda Byrne. I was thinking in my mind, *I need that book, seems like it would be interesting*. So I googled the title of the book then ordered it. I could not wait to receive it so that I could learn more things about life. Soon as I got it I started reading it. It was like receiving a present like a kid on Christmas day. Yes, I was that excited. I read that the secret to life is living by the law of attraction. Living by the law of attraction is all about your thoughts and feelings. The law of attraction is a natural law that determines the complete order of the universe and of our personal lives through the process of "like attracts like." The way this law is said to work is by attracting into a person's life the experiences, situations, events, and people that match the frequency of the person's thoughts and feelings. The book says thinking positively can create life-changing results such as increased wealth, health, and happiness. We create our own realities by our thoughts and actions.

Albert Einstein once said, "Everything is energy and that's all there is to it. Match the frequency of the reality you want and you cannot help but get the reality. It can be no other way." I believe that is true. For example, most of the thoughts I had in my mind were negative with bad feelings so I stayed on that frequency attracting more negative things into my life. That book made me realize that by thinking positive, being positive, and feeling good within I will continue to attract more positive things within my life. In the process of rewiring my brain I had to realize my thoughts, intentions, beliefs, and actions create my reality. I had to change some of my beliefs that I had about life in order to allow new beliefs to blossom in my life. I had to release my old doubts, fears, and perceived obstacles. For example, I would have a fear of speaking up or letting my voice be known. Now I know that I am a leader and by speaking up I can enlighten people in the world. I made the decision to stop letting my old beliefs prevent change from happening in my life. I have a growth mindset. With this kind of mindset I am more likely to maximize my potential, develop my skills, grow, and expand. Attempting to rewire my brain can be a tough process, but it is worth doing.

The Chosen One

In certain moments of my life I used to have regrets. It seemed like a lot of things were going wrong. I was going in circles because I was resisting change. When I stopped resisting change and just let it happen my life started to change in a good way. I started to see the light in life and live in it instead of the dark. I was alive but it was like I was not living. I was sleep, but now I am awakened to the world. When I put God first my life took a turn for the better. He was waiting on me all along. He is so amazing and is everything to me. To have a relationship with God is the best thing that could have ever happened to me. Without Him I would not be where I am today. He has moved a lot of negative things and baggage out of my life. He has removed certain people from my life so that they could not bring me down. God knows who belongs in my life and who does not. I trusted in Him and let go so that He could do his job. Whoever is meant to be a part of my life will still be in it. Sometimes the people around me will not understand my journey; they do not need to because it is not for them.

God has filled me with a great amount of wisdom, love, compassion, joy, courage, and faith. He continues to fill me with those things daily. The wisdom He provides me with is to enlighten others in the world so they can become awakened. Having faith in God means a lot to me. Having faith will take you a long way. God's messages to me are eye-opening. He is always trying to give us signs to guide us in life. If you do not believe in His work you might miss those signs. I believe in God and I am open to His work. Everything I went through in my life was for a reason. Anything I am going through right now is for a reason. I have no regrets about life. Where I am today is no accident. God is using the situation I am in right now to shape and prepare me for the place He wants to bring me into, which will be my big moment. I trust Him with His plan even if at times I do not understand it. That is the whole point of having faith.

CHAPTER 12
KNOWLEDGE IS POWER

When we gain knowledge we open up new opportunities for ourselves. When we educate ourselves and learn new things that we were unaware of that gives us the ability to make better decisions, come up with evolved and intelligent thoughts, and improve our lives and those around us. This makes us out to be more valuable people. The more valuable a person you are, the more people you will attract in your life. Those people may want to work with you, introduce you to people who need your help, and help you, and more doors and opportunities open in your life. Knowledge becomes part of who you are. To have the power of knowledge you have the freedom to speak your mind and to be who you truly are. You have the advantage of knowing information others may not know. You can use what you know or gain to your advantage. Knowledge is something that nobody can ever take away from you. Once you gain it that can transform the way you view the world. The more you learn, the more insights you can build on top of the things you already know. I gained knowledge from the lessons I learned in my life. Most of my knowledge was gained through the experiences I had. Once I learned from what I was doing wrong or what I did not understand it became my knowledge. I am using my knowledge and wisdom to my advantage to write this book. I want to enlighten you more about my life story. I want to provide you with some information to keep in mind as you are going through life.

The first thing you can keep in mind is to love yourself first. No one can love you like you can. When you love yourself first, then you can love others genuinely. When you are love you draw it toward you. You have to be love to receive real love. You attract what you are, stated by the law of attraction. Know your self-worth: If you do not know it no one else will. It is up to you to know what you do and do not deserve. You do not have to settle for less. When I started loving myself first I changed as a person. I embraced my flaws and everything else about me. I stopped being so hard on myself and started being kind to myself. I did not let people run over me as they had done in my past. I realized my self-worth and stopped putting up with anything less than what I deserved. It is best to heal yourself before dealing with others. If you do not you will carry baggage from your past relationships into your next one. Give yourself time for your wounds to heal. Give yourself time to learn from the past events that occurred in your life. Learn from it then move on. I was the kind of person to leave one relationship broken, then go to the next one without letting myself heal from the pain I encountered. I was not relationship ready, but I jumped in them anyway. I just tried to cover my pain, then tried to start a relationship to take my mind off the last person. All the pain was balled up within me from my past relationships or relations with people. So heal before dealing so that pain will not be built up inside of you. Keeping pain built up inside of you hurts you even more. You may not see it but you are becoming more damaged. It is never too late to fix yourself.

The second thing you can keep in mind is to know that your past affects your future. You cannot change what happened in your past, but you can work in your present to have a better future. The past can come back to haunt you. For example, if you have treated people badly in your past the way you treated them will come back on you. Create good karma instead of bad karma. It is never too late to start creating good karma. When I held grudges toward people who hurt me from the past I was hurting myself. I was holding myself back, playing the victim. I learned how to forgive them and move on. I realized the reason why my parents did not express their feelings to us is because it was the way they were raised. They did not express themselves to their parents going up. I was not able to express myself to them like I wanted to. This was a generational issue. The past has affected my parents and me. I forgave them for not being able to teach me how to express myself more to them. They were not taught how to, so I cannot blame them. I started teaching myself the things I did not know. That part about me not being able to express myself in my past affected me in my future because I would hold everything in without expressing myself. I was suppressing my feelings. When I learned that suppressing feelings is not healthy for a person I started expressing myself more in life. It is a good thing to release your pain, fears, doubts, and perceived obstacles that are from your past. It can be a process, but anything is possible.

The third thing that you can keep in mind is to not be afraid to change. It is possible that you can change your life around at any moment. If you believe you can, then you will make the effort to. In this book I talk to you about how my past was and how I changed as a person. Anything you put your mind to you can do. That is what I did and I accomplished a lot by doing that. I have been underestimated my whole life by lots of people. I ended up proving them wrong by putting my mind to everything that I did. Be open to change if you are ready to change. You cannot be willing to change with a closed mind — it does not work that way. When you become more open-minded you are open to new ways that you might have to adjust to. You will see the world differently from the way you used to see it when you were close-minded. When I became more open-minded I was able to expand my knowledge.

I saw things about myself that needed to be worked on and changed. Being stagnant in life gets you nowhere. I was at a point in my life where I got fed up of doing the same things and being the same person. I felt like it was time for me to grow and expand. That was the best thing that I could do for myself. When you do decide to change it comes to a point where you will have to let the old you go, so you can become the new you. The old you will no longer serve. Your life will change completely when you change the way you think, things you do that may have a bad effect on you, negative thoughts you have, certain things you watch on television, certain songs you listen to with bad intent, and bad influences around you. For example, if you are used to being around people who don't have anything going for themselves and you don't either you are not going to want to do better as long as you continue to be around them. When you separate yourself from them and surround yourself with people who have something going for themselves you will want better for yourself too.

You have to understand that your thoughts, intentions, beliefs, and actions create your reality. For example, if you continue to think negatively about yourself and the things around you that only puts out more negative results. Change your thought patterns to positive thoughts and your results will be better. You can change your thought process around, and that will become your reality. Once I started thinking and being positive, life became better for me. Think and be positive; your life will change for the better. Your thoughts are real if you believe it or not. The words you speak are being put out into the universe and becoming real. So be aware of your thinking patterns and the words you say.

The fourth thing that you can keep in mind is to know that you are who you are. If you're lost about knowing who you are I suggest that you start finding yourself. Focus on the things about you. Pay attention to the way you think, do things, say things, what you like, do not like, your traits, characteristics, strengths, and weaknesses. Another thing you can do is ask for guidance from God or whoever you praise. When you are lost start being true and honest to yourself. When you do that you will not have to live a lie. You will be honest to the ones around you. For example, when I was lost I did not have anyone to turn to for help — most of them were lost themselves too. I had to find my own way. I started focusing on me and who I was. I was teaching myself stuff on my own. In the process I asked for guidance from God. I started to pray every night. The more I prayed the more things changed and I became aware. When I became aware I was awakened to myself and the world around me.

Do not let anyone change the real you. When someone gives you advice you can take it or leave it. It is all up to you. Do not let people's opinions change or sway you in the wrong direction. You have to trust in yourself to make the right choice for you. People are bashed all the time by others telling them, "You are not like others," "You should be this way," or "You are weird." So what if you are weird and not like others? Stand out, embrace your flaws, and take pride in who you are! It is OK to do so. I have flaws that people would point out or do not approve of. I would get mad at myself for having them. I learned that was the wrong way to go about it. I learned how to embrace my flaws instead of bashing myself for having them. I could not help that God created me a certain way. I turned most of my flaws into strengths. The things about me are what make me who I am. Surround yourself with positive people who will uplift you and people who have something going for themselves. Those negative people will bring you down to their level.

You may have a sexual preference that others do not approve of. Whatever your sexual preference is do not be ashamed of it. When you are ashamed of it you are not able to be who you are. I understand what you are going through, so you are not alone. So come out about it and you will feel much better. People have kept theirs a secret for years because of how people would judge them. People have committed suicide because their sexual preference was not accepted by their loved ones. Don't let that be you, be proud of who you are even if other people do not like it. It is your choice, your life, and not anyone else's. Live the life that you want to live instead of living the life someone else may want you to live. Take control of your own life. We are not meant to be perfect, we are meant to be whole.

The fifth thing that you can keep in mind is to know that everyone has a purpose on this earth. Once you know who you are you can identify your gifts. You can use those gifts that you were born with to start on the path of your purpose. At one point in my life I was having suicidal thoughts, I did not want to live anymore, felt less than everyone else around me, and thought I had no reason to be here on earth. I felt like no one understood or loved me. One day when I started my spiritual awakening my life changed. I have a lot to live for. There are many things in life to be grateful for. I had to realize that if no one understands me I know God does. He showed me that I have purpose here on earth. If I did not I would not be here. It was a wake-up call for me. Never think you are not worth anything; you are worth something. If you are feeling unloved, know that God loves you and someone else out there does too. You have a reason to be living; you have your life to live for family, friends, or kids. I know part of my purpose is to help people in life for different reasons. I enjoy learning and helping them with their issues. When I do it, it comes from the heart. I am passionate about that. It makes me happy to know that I can make someone else happy. By finding out what our purpose is here on earth we can all make the world a better place.

The sixth thing that you can keep in mind is that you can be the chosen one too. Being the chosen one is the path to tapping into your life purpose to make the world a better place. The choice is yours if you want to or not. God chooses the ones who allow Him to work in them. He chooses people who are looked over by others. You have to be able to let Him use you and have an open mind. I am starting to tap into my life purpose. This is the path I am choosing to be on. If you choose to be on that path to pursue your life's purpose you have to pay attention to God's signs and signs of the universe. Everything happens for a reason. Everyone is special; you just have to believe it within your heart. Do not be afraid to tap into your purpose and live up to God's plan that He made for you. There are going to be people you come across who do not understand your purpose — it is not for them to understand. Keep doing what you are supposed to be doing for your life's purpose. By telling your story in life I am sure you can help, change, and save people's lives too. Be a leader and not a follower. When I was lost in the world all I did was follow other people, not knowing that God wanted me to step out on my own and be a leader myself. I would sit in the background of everything I was involved in. I was the one with the knowledge. Now that I know my value and my purpose God has chosen me out of the crowd to be a leader.

I have brought a lot of things to your attention that you may be faced with in your life or you have already experienced. I did not get to cover everything because we know that there are more things to be informed about in life. I hope that the information I did mention made an impact on your life. You can use my knowledge that I provided you with to your advantage to improve yourself and others around you.

IN CLOSING

⌇⌇

I hope my book has helped you in some way. Hopefully you can find ways in the things you have experienced in your life to relate to my life situations. I am trying to get a message out to others to never give up on life no matter how broken you are, what you have been through, how hard it may be, or how damaged you may be. Remember that you can always be healed. The first step to healing is to accept the fact that you are damaged, then seek help. The more you stay in denial about yourself the more you will be damaged. Once you get the help you need you have to make the choice to change or not. You have to be open about things in life if you want to change yourself. It is never too late to change. Never let anyone change you from being who you are meant to be. I am talking about your true self, not someone you pretend to be — there is a difference. If people have a problem with you being your true self, they talk about you, bring you down, and pick on you. Let them — who cares what they think? You have to live that life, they do not. People will talk about you till the day you leave this earth and maybe afterward too. Let them talk; you cannot control other people. Only person you can control is yourself. Live the life you want to live. We only get one life to live. Make the best of it. Take the initiative in your life to become a better you and your life will change for the better. I am doing it as of right now by writing this book. This book has brought out things in me and parts of my life that I see I can work on more. There is always more room to grow and expand. When you are not growing and expanding in some way to become a better person you are being stagnant. Stagnant people get nowhere in life. Their life is like a circle and they continue to go through the same things. They will continue to go through the same things because they will not change in order to grow. Most people are afraid to change because of the fear of losing something in their lives. That may happen, but whatever you lose from change will be worth losing if it is for the better.

Remember that fear hinders the heart, love conquers all. So let your heart be filled with love instead of fear. Let go of those old doubts and fears so that you can live a free life. You have to know that your fears and doubts hold you back. Do not let them hold you back in life. Keep faith. It might not seem like things are getting easier, but faith makes them possible. Believe in yourself: What we believe shapes who we are. My awakening experience shifted my whole life. I got in touch with my spiritual side. Now that my life has been changed I have decided that I will not be going back to who I used to be. When I chose to start my life over I started with a new pattern of thoughts, wave of emotions, connection to the world, and belief system. It took courage to tell you my life story filled with mind-blowing experiences and secrets. The book made a way for me to express who I am, learn more things about myself, and help others. I am blossoming into my true self and stepping into my life's purpose. I hope you have been encouraged to do the same. Know that we are all connected as people. We are made up of energy. We are all on a journey together. We are a part of God. God is within all of us; He is our creator. Be grateful and mindful of life. See your life as a class so that you can learn from it.

The Chosen One,
Brittany Carson